Contents

Progress tracker

Colour the place name for each letter you complete.

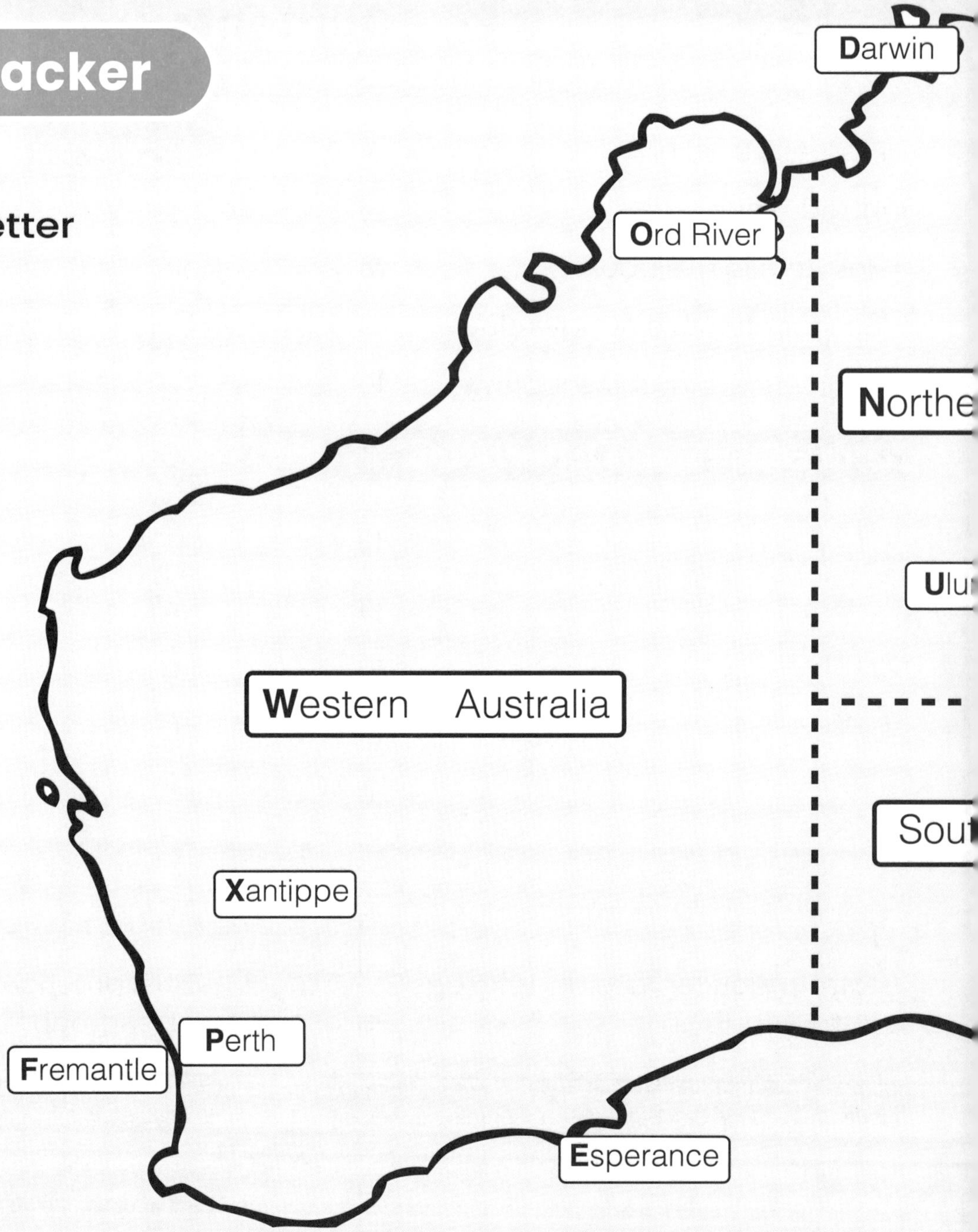

X marks the place of a mystery city. Work out the name of the city as you complete the letter pages.

The mystery city is ______________________________.

Add your suburb or town to the map.

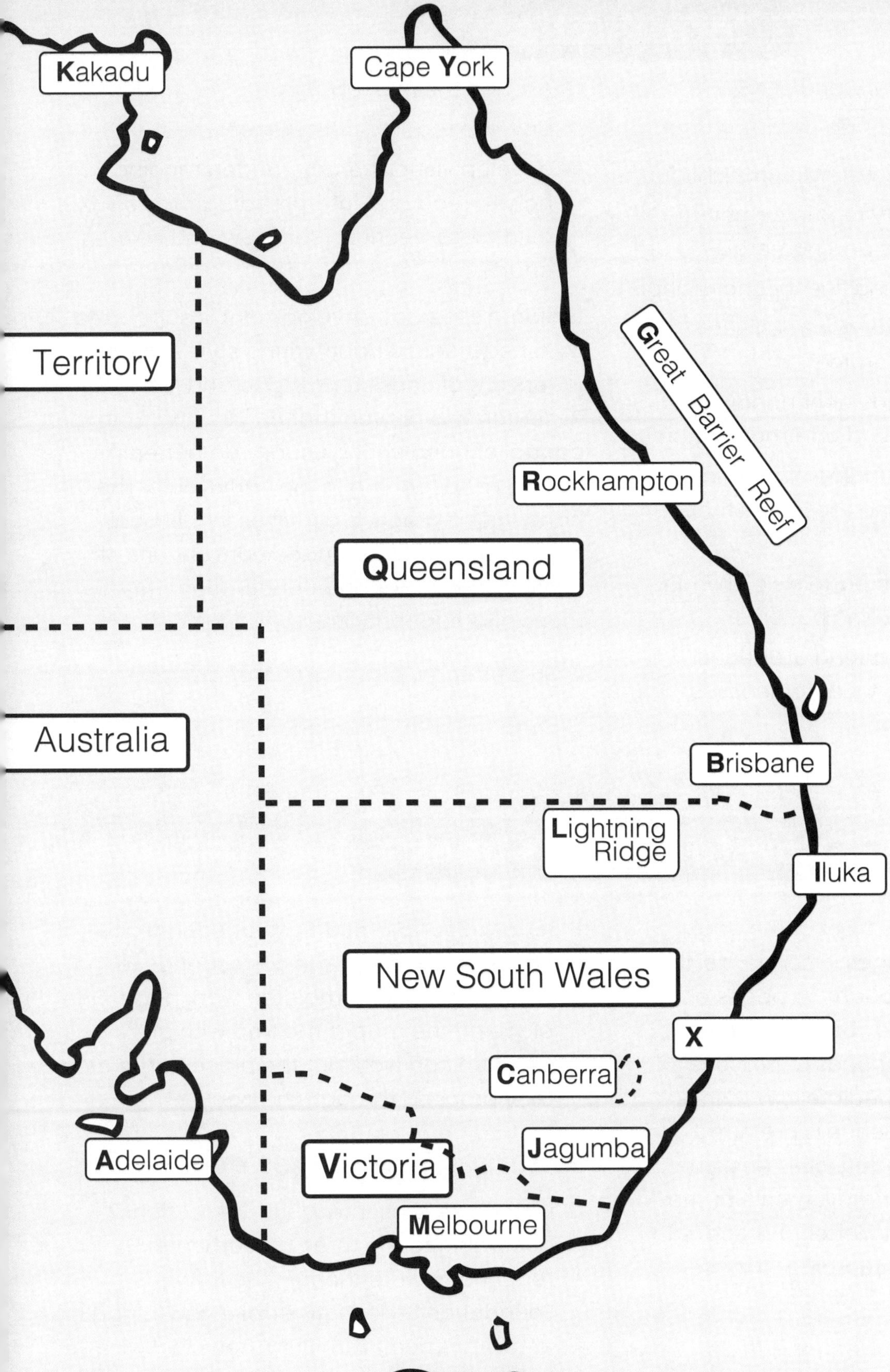

Kakadu
Cape York
Territory
Great Barrier Reef
Rockhampton
Queensland
Australia
Brisbane
Lightning Ridge
Iluka
New South Wales
X
Canberra
Adelaide
Victoria
Jagumba
Melbourne
Tasmania
Zeehan
Hobart

Introduction

Welcome to the wonderful world of NSW Foundation Style handwriting.

The activities in this book will help your child:

- consolidate their ability to print upper- and lower-case letters and numerals
- develop neat, legible and fluent handwriting
- improve their fine motor control, visual discrimination and coordination
- learn to value neat and fluent handwriting as an effective method of communication
- develop their understanding of phonics—the sounds in words and the letters that spell those sounds
- develop their ability to create lists of rhyming words with different spelling patterns
- develop their understanding of various aspects of grammar (nouns, adjectives, verbs) and punctuation
- expand their vocabulary
- develop reading comprehension skills
- develop visual literacy (understanding how to read and interpret diagrams such as a cross-section, plan view and flow chart).

Children's literacy development is supported by a neat, legible handwriting style, where letters are of consistent shape and size. Research has proven that children with good control of handwriting usually do better in spelling and reading in the early years. The handwriting practice activities in this book are based on the language conventions of spelling, grammar and punctuation. This focus also supports literacy learning.

As in all things, practice makes perfect!

How to use this book

Children can begin at the front of the book and work through the pages in sequence. It is also possible to work through the pages out of sequence according to your child's needs; for example, if your child needs to practise specific letters more immediately. Working through the book in sequence is preferred, however, because the sequence is designed to focus on the particular movements of the NSW Foundation Style and letter practice is sequenced in the book according to those movements.

Progress tracker

- The progress tracker on pages 4 and 5 is a quick reference that you can use to check your child's progress through the letters. Your child can colour each place name on the map that corresponds to the focus letter of a completed work page. One place on the map is marked with an X. Children can work out the place name as they proceed through the book.

Letter practice pages overview

- Letters are presented in three sections according to the three movements required to write them in the NSW Foundation Style. Downstroke and zigzag letters are dealt with first, then clockwise letters and finally anticlockwise letters. Each section is followed by a number of extra practice pages that reinforce the particular movement.

- Each letter is presented across a double-page spread. Lower-case and upper-case versions of each letter are covered simultaneously with lines of practice for each and then words to trace and copy. These words include the focus letter.
- At the bottom of each page is a parent tip. As well as handwriting reminders and problems to watch for, the tips include spelling, grammar and punctuation teaching points or suggestions and activities, and other information for parents.

Left-hand letter page

The left-hand letter page includes:

- A row of lower-case letters and a row of upper-case letters for students to trace.
- A row of start dots to support students as they write the focus lower-case letter across the writing lines, then a row of start dots to support students as they write the focus upper-case letter across the writing lines.
- Two, three or four words to trace and add the missing focus letter, then a set of blank lines for student to write the words independently. These words help students learn phonics and reinforce their understanding of spelling patterns.
- The common words are drawn from the 1000 most common words that students need to learn how to spell; for example, usually, sure, while. These words cannot be spelt phonetically or by using the strategy of 'sounding out'. Children need to know how to spell these common words so they can use them when writing and they need to learn to automatically recognise them when they read them, rather than try to sound them out.
- A parent tip that may include reminders about aspects of handwriting but that also draws attention to such things as spelling patterns, rhyme, phonics and letter–sound correspondences.

The tracking, tracing and independent practice activities make use of the guidelines on the page. Guidelines help your child learn to write letters of consistent size relative to each other. Start dots help with letter spacing and word spacing, as well as showing the starting point of each letter.

Right-hand letter page

The right-hand letter page includes:

- Practice opportunities to trace the focus lower- and upper-case pairs of letters.
- A diagram with labels. Students can colour the diagram and trace the labels and headings. These labels and headings are not within writing lines in order to support your child's practice at writing smaller-sized letters. The diagrams are varied and can be humorous or factual. The factual diagrams support other learning areas such as science. The types of diagrams include a plan view, cross-section, flow chart and life cycle.
- A sentence accompanies each diagram. The sentence could be factual and objective or emotive and subjective. Suggestions are given in the parent tips to build on your child's understanding of texts, punctuation and grammar as well as spelling. Children can explore the various sentence structures as well as the associated punctuation markers. The sentences reinforce the use of upper-case letters to begin sentences and people's names (proper nouns).

- The parent tip on each right-hand page provides support for parents in the following areas: visual literacy (reading and understanding diagrams), grammar, spelling, vocabulary and punctuation.

Extra letter practice

After each set of pages dealing with one of the three handwriting movements (straight lines and zigzags, clockwise and then anticlockwise) there are extra practice pages where words previously introduced on the letter pages are repeated in alphabetical order. The blank lines help parents determine whether their child is beginning each letter correctly, positioning the letters on and within the writing lines correctly and spacing letters and words correctly.

These pages have parent tips that support spelling, as well as handwriting tips that suggest things to watch for as you observe your child engaged in writing (e.g. pencil grip, a relaxed style, fluency and legibility).

Use the word lists for reading practice (make flash cards or games such as Snap) or use the lists for spelling practice. Expand the lists as you explore more words with your child.

Numeral practice pages

The six numeral practice pages (pages 79–84) cover numerals, ordinal numbers and words for numbers, including hundred and thousand.

Text pages

There are nine pages that allow for revision and consolidation. They can also be used for assessment purposes. Six of these pages include a text sample in small font at the top of the page. Students need to copy the text correctly onto the writing lines. Because no support is provided for your child on these pages you can observe your child and note aspects of their writing such as fluency, legibility, speed, accuracy, letters of consistent size and shape, letters beginning and ending correctly according to the movement required, and the position of letters on the writing lines, as well as the punctuation marks. A number of the texts are not organised into specific lines for copying. Your child will need to judge whether a whole word will fit on a line before they start writing it.

The final revision pages include a questionnaire. Children are required to fill in the answers in their neatest handwriting without the support of writing guidelines. These pages will show parents whether their child understands the concept of the placement of letters in relation to each other.

Tips for effective handwriting

- The poster on page 96 can be used by your child as a reminder of the three Ps of posture, pencil grip and paper/page tilt. It can also help them develop self-correcting skills.

The three Ps for right-handed writers

The three Ps are:

Posture

- Remind your child to sit with a straight back and with both feet flat on the floor.

Paper tilt

- The writing paper should be tilted correctly with the top right up. The left hand can hold the paper or book in place.

Pencil grip

- Reinforce a correct grip as early as possible in your child's life so that incorrect or awkward habits don't form in the first place. Tell your child to hold the pencil 2 cm from the tip between their index finger and their thumb with its shaft in the open web between index finger and thumb. The pencil rests on the middle finger. The heel of the writing hand rests on the page so the writing hand is steady.
- Use large soft-leaded pencils to begin with. Make sure writing implements are not slippery as these are more difficult to grip. You could also buy a rubber grip for your child's pencil. It can be used to help your child maintain a correct grip.

The three Ps for left-handed writers

- Ten per cent of people are left-handed and more boys than girls are left-handed.
- Being left-handed does not mean your child will have messy handwriting. It just means they will have a few extra challenges to overcome because the world is largely set up for right-handed people.

Posture

- Remind your child to sit with a straight back and with both feet flat on the floor.

Paper tilt

- Tilt the page left corner up and right side down so they can see the tip of the pencil and where they are writing. Tell them to use their right hand to hold the page steady. Use a start dot on the left side of the page to remind your child where to start.

Pencil grip

- Have your child hold their pencil 2 to 3 cm from the tip. This is close enough to the tip to give them good control of the pencil but far enough away from the tip that they can see their writing.
- Make sure the shaft of the pencil rests in the web of the hand between the thumb and forefinger.
- Left-handed writers have to *push* their pencil rather than *pull* their pencil, so it is more difficult. Pulling is smoother and easier than pushing. Pushing means you are more likely to tear the paper or smudge the writing.

- Tell your child not to press too hard. Buying them pencils with softer lead will also help prevent paper tearing. Softer lead allows for softer pressure and also helps avoid hand strain. Pencils with broader tips are easier than fine tips, which tend to tear the page more readily.
- Avoid marking pens with ink that stays wet because it can smudge as your child's hand moves over it as they write.
- The grip should be relaxed and not hooked or cramped. Make sure your child keeps their wrist straight. This will avoid cramping but also allow your child to see their writing. They need to keep their hand below the writing line.
- Practising on a vertical chalkboard or whiteboard can help free up arm movements.

TIP Check that your child's classroom allows for a left-hand computer mouse and left-handed scissors.

Sitting on the left

- In any situation where two children are sharing a desk or table for writing, the **left-handed child** should sit **on the left side** of the right-handed child so they don't bump arms when writing. Make sure there's space on the left to support the child's left arm.

Handwriting troubleshooting

- Handwriting is important for writing. When handwriting is slow and laboured, and when children have trouble reading their own handwriting, it leads to frustration and embarrassment at school. Children then avoid handwriting and it becomes a vicious cycle. Without practice they can't improve. Achieving success from the very beginning is important in supporting children's confidence as writers. Efficient handwriting helps students get their thoughts on to paper quickly and their creativity can flow. Most children can improve their handwriting with practice and targeted intervention but some may always struggle.
- Parents can help identify issues early on before children's self-esteem is affected to prevent the impact that poor handwriting has on other areas of learning.

IMPORTANT Do not despair if your child has poor handwriting. Your child can improve with practice. Make practice fun and rewarding and use other activities to support the various other skills that are beneficial for aspects of handwriting such as fine motor control and visual discrimination.

Watch your child as they write

- How do they look? Comfortable or uncomfortable? Relaxed or tense?
- What are their wrists, arms, shoulders, fingers, etc. doing as they write?

Look at the writing your child is producing

- Are the letters cramped, of irregular sizes or illegible?

Talk to your child about handwriting

- Ask them how they feel about writing. Do they enjoy it or avoid it? Do they value handwriting as a skill? If they find writing difficult, does it bother them? Are they worried about their handwriting? Do they care about handwriting? Have they seen you write to understand the importance of legible handwriting?

Handwriting problems can occur in these main areas:

Issue	What's needed	How to help
Speed and fluency	If they are too slow, it indicates that your child cannot write the letters without thinking; they are needing to concentrate to try to recall what they need to do.	Your child needs to develop automaticity (where writing letters and the letter sequences useful in phonics becomes automatic and they don't have to think about it).
Letter shapes and legibility	Muscle memory and automaticity	Practise movements and the shapes.
	Knowledge of where letters start and end, that letters in words are of uniform size and that words need to be planned and their lengths estimated so they don't run into each other or run off the end of the line	Practise identifying letters, their differences and similarities, including where each starts and finishes on the guidelines and its position in relation to the letter that precedes it in words. Describe the letters as your child writes them to draw on auditory memory as well as visual and motor memory about where letters start and finish and their movements.
Letters not sitting correctly on lines	Knowledge about where each letter begins and finishes on the guidelines	Point out tall letters and long letters and which letters only have a body and no head or tail and where these aspects of the letters sit on the guidelines. Practise.
Slope	Understanding that a consistent slope is required so that letters do not run into each other or look cramped	Practise forming letters of consistent and regular slope.
Uneven and/or inconsistent space between letters and between words	Understanding how letters are formed, especially anticlockwise letters, so that enough space is left after a letter so that the following letter does not overlap it or encroach upon its space; for example, any letter followed by *o*, *a* or *e* Recognition that spaces exist between words and that, in English, writing moves from left to right	Practise writing and then reading what is written.
Mixing upper-case and lower-case letters	This is normal in young children but if it continues into Year 2 seek professional advice. Provide practice opportunities for your child to learn to differentiate the letters.	Do activities to develop visual discrimination.
Reversals (writing letters and numerals back to front)	This is normal up until the age of about eight. If it continues, seek professional advice.	Use auditory and visual memory triggers; for example, tell your child that *b* looks a bit like a bat next to a ball. So for *b* say 'First the *bat* then the *ball*'.
Pencil grip and pressure	The correct grip is essential for relaxed and fluid writing (see page 96). Pencil tips that aren't broken	Make sure pencils, paper or other writing surface is appropriate for your child's stage of development.
Posture or body position	Correct positioning of wrist, arm, neck and shoulders, feet and paper is necessary to avoid pressure, hand cramps, discomfort or neck strain.	Sit correctly (check the PPP poster on page 96). Do warm-ups and stretching.
Inconsistent formation of letters	Impact on spelling	When letters in words look different each time a child writes them, it's hard for the child to develop any visual memory for the way the words should look or to develop any muscle memory for how it feels to write the word. This can affect your child's spelling.

Practice

Trace

l l l l l l

L L L L L L

Write

l l

L L

Write the missing l's. Trace the words. Copy the words.

wa k ta k cha k wa k

rea ly a most s owly

PARENT TIP: Discuss rhyme: *walk*, *talk*, *chalk*. Point out how to add suffixes (*walked*, *walks*, *walking*) where possible. Use the common spelling words in sentences. Have your child practise the spelling.

Practice

Trace

Il Il Il Il Il Il

Trace the labels. Colour the diagram.

Flowering Plant

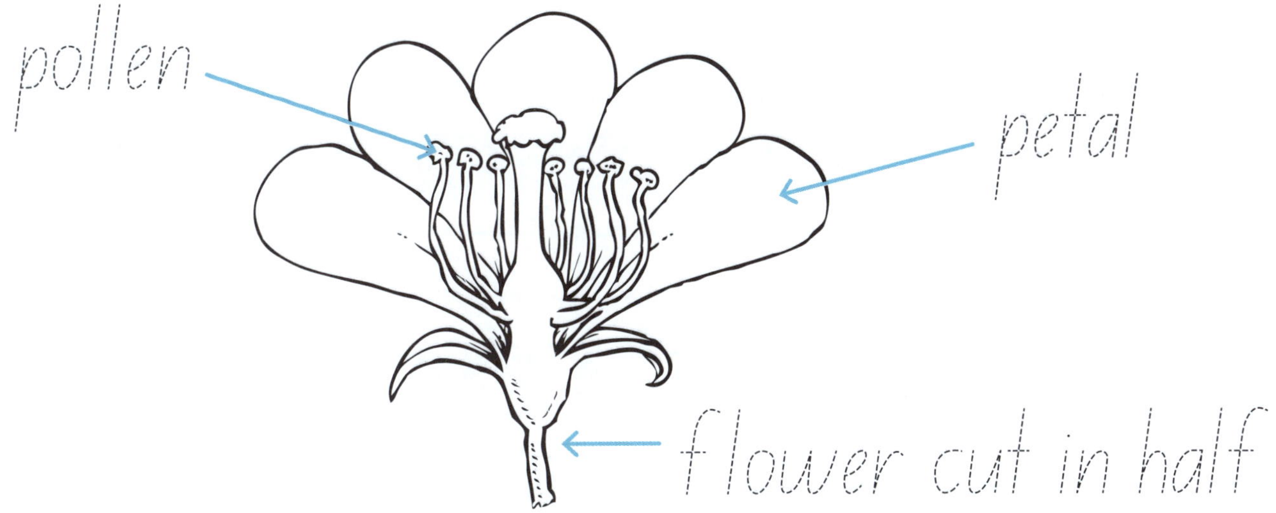

Write the sentence.

A flower has petals and pollen.

PARENT TIP: The diagram is a cross-section. Point out that cross-sections are often used in scientific diagrams. Have your child read the sentence. The sentence makes a statement of fact. The word *has* is a being and having (relating) verb. Ask your child to identify the common nouns in the statement (*flower*, *petals*, *pollen*).

Practice

Trace

t t t t t t

T T T T T T

Write

t t

T T

Write the missing t's. Trace the words. Copy the words.

bo tle bee le li tle bo tle

hose be ter lis en hose

PARENT TIP: Make sure your child crosses the T and t from left to right. Point out the -le at the end of the first three words. Brainstorm other words with that spelling pattern at the end: *throttle*, *startle*, *rattle*, *steeple*, *people*, *thistle*, etc. Discuss words that rhyme with *those*, including words with different spelling patterns: *nose*, *hose*, *chose*, *toes*, *rows*, *grows*, *throws*. Point out the silent t in *listen*.

Practice

Trace

ff ff ff ff ff ff

Trace the labels. Colour the diagram.

Parts of an Ant

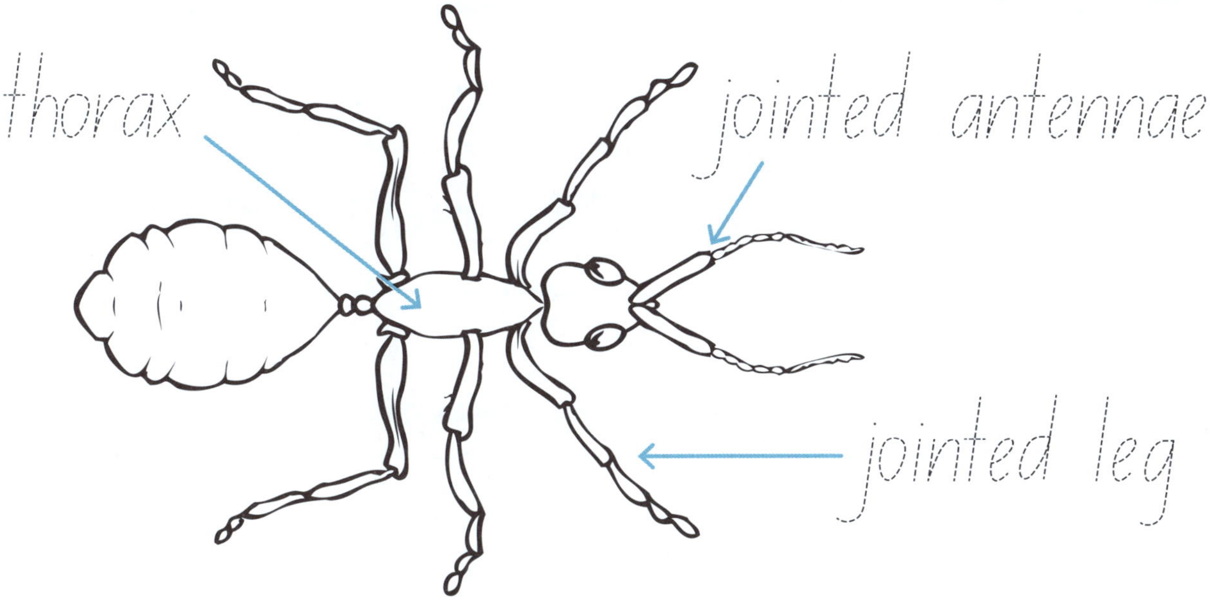

Write the sentence.

An ant is an insect with legs that are jointed.

PARENT TIP: Point out the scientific diagram and the specific terminology used to label the body parts (*thorax*, *antennae*). Explain that the singular word is *antenna*. Ask your child to find small words in *antennae*, e.g. *ant*, *ten*.

Practice

Trace

i i i i i i

I I I I I I

Write

i i

I I

Write the missing *i*'s. Trace the words. Copy the words.

sh rt c rcle th rteen

'll mportant dea 'll

PARENT TIP: Discuss the *ir* spelling pattern in the first three words and the single sound the two letters make. Point out that other letter combinations make the same sound: *burn*, *pearl*, *work*, *her*. Ensure your child writes an upper-case *I* in *I'll*. Point out that the contraction uses an apostrophe to mark the place of the letters *wi* which have been left out of *I will*.

Practice

Trace

il il il il il il

Trace the labels. Colour the diagram.

Ingredients to Make Icing

Write the sentence.

I like making icing. It is delicious!

PARENT TIP: Make the contraction *It's* from *It is*. Discuss the emotive personal opinion statements in the text. The thinking/feeling verb *like* expresses a positive opinion and the adjective *delicious* also expresses a positive opinion.

Practice

Trace

x x x x x x

X X X X X X

Write

x x

X X

Write the missing *x*'s. Trace the words. Copy the words.

letterbo chickenpo bo

e ample e citing e treme

PARENT TIP: Make sure that your child begins this letter with the first stroke starting at the top left and moving down and the second stroke starting at the bottom left and moving up. Point out that the *x* makes the sound /*ks*/ in words such as *box*. *Letterbox* and *chickenpox* are compound words. This means they are two words joined together to make a new word with a new meaning.

Practice

Trace

xX xX xX xX xX xX

Trace the labels. Colour the diagram.

Write the sentence.

This chatterbox ox is wearing sox.

PARENT TIP: Discuss the humour in the illustration and the text. Talk about the words in the speech bubble that use *x*. Make lists of words using *ax*, *ex*, *ix*, *ox*, *ux*. Discuss the meaning of the word *tux* which is short for *tuxedo*.

Practice

Trace

z z z z z z

Z Z Z Z Z Z

Write

z z

Z Z

Write the missing *z*'s. Trace the words. Copy the words.

fi z ero bu z fi z

si e free e fro en si e

PARENT TIP: Check that your child's posture is correct. Discuss words with a single z and double zz. Point out the z in the middle of words included on the page. Do an internet search for words with z in the middle, e.g. *buzzard*.

Practice

Trace

z Z z Z z Z z Z z Z z Z

Trace the labels. Colour the diagram.

Zac the Zebra

Write the sentence.

Zac the zebra is jazzy at the zoo.

PARENT TIP: Discuss the humour in the illustration. Talk about *jazzy* as an adjective and what it means in the illustration; that is, colourful or showy. *Zac* is a proper noun.

Practice

Trace

f f f f f f

F F F F F F

Write

f f

F F

Write the missing f's. Trace the words. Copy the words.

irst ive our irst

ast amily riends ast

PARENT TIP: Make sure your child crosses the *f* from left to right. This is important for linking letters in Year 3. Make sure your child knows the difference between *for* and *four*. Create lists of words that rhyme with *for* or *four*; for example, *your*, *door*, *pore*, *pour*, *paw*, *oar*. Point out the silent *i* in *friends*.

Practice

Trace

f F f F f F f F f F f F

Trace the labels. Colour the diagram.

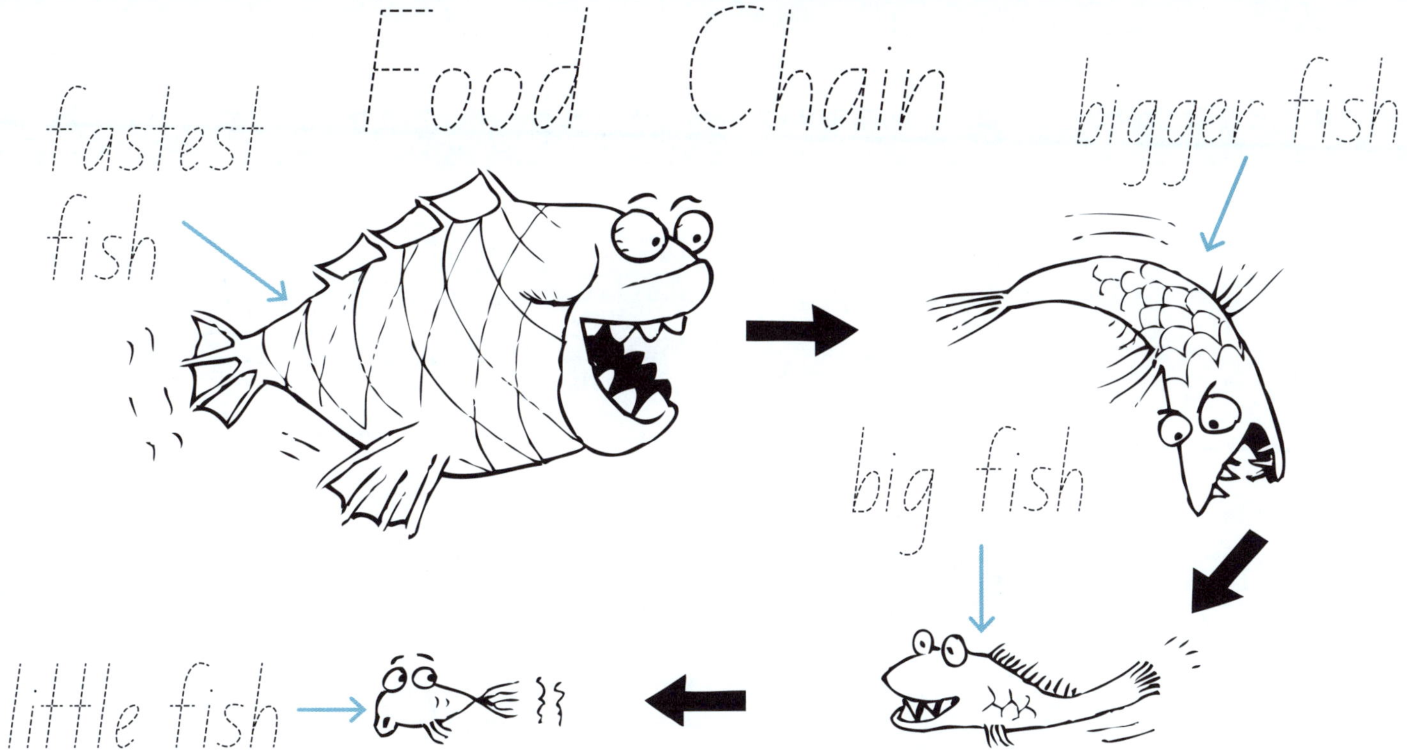

Write the sentence.

Energy from food flows up the food chain.

PARENT TIP: Watch that your child's writing style is fluent and comfortable and that they are using the correct grip. The diagram is a flow chart. The sentence explains what the flow chart shows. Discuss the concepts shown in the chart.

Practice

Trace

j j j j j j
j j j j j j

Write

j j
j j

Write the missing *j*'s. Trace the words. Copy the words.

uggle iggle angle

umped ust ob ect ug

PARENT TIP: Point out the -*gle* ending on some of the words. Explore rhyming words for each spelling pattern: *struggle*; *wriggle*; *dangle*, *bangle*, *tangle*.

Practice

Trace

j j j j j j

Trace the labels. Colour the diagram.

Write the sentence.

The jaguar was joyful to be back in the jungle.

PARENT TIP: Discuss the humour in the illustration. Ask where the *jaguar* might have been. Make up a story that tells of the *jaguar*'s adventures.

Extra practice: lines and zigzags

Write the words.

almost antennae

beetle better bottle

box butter buzz

chalk chickenpox

circle delicious

example exciting family

PARENT TIP: These pages support revision of zigzag and downstroke handwriting movements. The words are in alphabetical order. Read through the words with your child. Discuss spelling patterns; for example, the sound made by the letters *al* in *chalk*; the sound made by the letter *c* in *exciting*. Write words that rhyme with the *ox* sound: *sox*, *ox*, *clocks*, *rocks*, *flocks*.

Extra practice: lines and zigzags

Write the words.

fast first fish

five fizz flower

flows food four

freeze friends from

frozen fuzz idea

I'll important

PARENT TIP: Point out the sound made by the letter *a* in *fast*. Discuss compound words such as *chickenpox* on the previous page. Start a list of compound words: *footpath*, *netball*, *playground*, *grandfather*, *grandmother*.

Extra practice: lines and zigzags

Write the words.

insect jangle jet

jingle joyous juggle

jumped jungle just

legs letterbox like

listen little milk

mix object parts

PARENT TIP: These pages revise zigzag and downstroke handwriting movements. The words are in alphabetical order. Read through the words with your child and discuss any noteworthy spelling patterns.

Extra practice: lines and zigzags

Write the words.

petal plant pollen

really shirt six

size slowly sox

tall thirteen thorax

those walk zebra

zero zigzag zoo

PARENT TIP: Ask your child to identify similarities between words on the page; for example, *shirt* and *thirteen* both include the *ir* spelling pattern; and *six*, *sox* and *thorax* contain the /*ks*/ sound made by *x*.

Practice

Trace

m m m m m m

M M M M M M

Write

m m

M M

Write the missing *m*'s. Trace the words. Copy the words.

fla e sa e ta e fla e

ight re e ber oney

PARENT TIP: Point out the initial downstroke and then the clockwise movement to make an *m*. Point out the rhyme in *flame*, *same*, *tame*. Think of other words which rhyme: *shame*, *blame*, *came*, *game*. Discuss the *igh* spelling pattern in *might*. Point out the *ey* spelling and the sound the letters make at the end of *money*.

Practice

Trace

mMmMmMmMmMmM

Trace the labels. Colour the diagram.

Write the sentence.

Make marvellous music with instruments.

PARENT TIP: Read the words with your child. Talk about the different musical instruments. Search for them on the internet to hear the sounds they make.

Practice

Trace

n n n n n n

N N N N N N

Write

n n

N N

Write the missing *n*'s. Trace the words. Copy the words.

ear wro g oisy ear

ever ext ight ext

PARENT TIP: Point out the initial downstroke and then the clockwise movement to make an *n*. Talk about the *ng* at the end of *wrong*. Compile a list of *ng* words; for example, *sing*, *song*, *thing*, *ring*, *rang*, *sing*. Point out the *igh* in *night* and the single sound the three letters make.

Practice

Trace

n N n N n N n N n N n N

Trace the labels. Colour the diagram.

Write the sentence.

A nosy neighbour is not nice.

PARENT TIP: Talk about the word *nosy* as an adjective. Point out the single sound made by the letters *eigh* in *neighbour* as well as the letters *our* at the end of the word.

Practice

Trace

r r r r r r

R R R R R R

Write

r • • • • r

R • • • • R

Write the missing *r*'s. Trace the words. Copy the words.

mo e cho e sco e mo e

o de doo sho t doo

PARENT TIP: Point out the initial downstroke and then the clockwise movement to make an *r*. Discuss the rhyme in *more*, *chore*, *score*. Other words which rhyme have different spelling patterns: *floor*, *chore*, *gnaw*, *boar*. Point out that the word *order* has two *r*'s.

Practice

Trace

rR rR rR rR rR rR

Trace the labels. Colour the diagram.

Write the sentence.

The bear crossed the raging river.

PARENT TIP: Discuss the meaning of *rapids* and *raging*. Tell your child that *bear* and *bare* are homophones. Homophones are words that sound the same but that have different spellings and meanings.

Practice

Trace

h h h h h h

H H H H H H

Write

h h

H H

Write the missing *h*'s. Trace the words. Copy the words.

s iver s ape s ow

ard our w ole ard

PARENT TIP: Point out the initial downstroke and then the clockwise movement that begins halfway back up the downstroke of the *h*. Your child should not lift their pencil to form this letter. Tell your child that *hour* has the word *our* in it. Make sure they understand the meanings of *hole* and *whole*. These words are examples of homophones.

Practice

Trace

h h h h h h h h h h h h

Trace the labels. Colour the diagram.

Write the sentence.

The itchy chimp scratched its hairy chin.

PARENT TIP: Ask your child to point out every letter *h* in the words. Some have their own sound as in *hop*. Some have a combined sound with other letters, e.g. *ch* in *chimp* and *chin*. Sometimes *h* makes no sound, e.g. the final *h* in *high*.

Practice

Trace

b b b b b b

B B B B B B

Write

b b

B B

Write the missing *b*'s. Trace the words. Copy the words.

reak rake rittle

egin a ove ecome

PARENT TIP: The letter *b* begins with a downstroke and then moves back up the stroke to commence the clockwise movement. Ask your child to identify the homophones on the page and tell you the meaning of each word. Discuss the meaning of *brittle*.

Practice

Trace

b B b B b B b B b B b B

Trace the labels. Colour the diagram.

Bee Ballet

Write the sentence.

The busy bumblebee buzzed about the bush.

PARENT TIP: Watch that your child's writing style is fluent and comfortable and they are using a relaxed, correct pencil grip. Discuss the illustration and what the *bee* is doing (collecting pollen). Have your child trace the twirling lines as well as the words.

Practice

Trace

p p p p p p

P P P P P P

Write

p p

P P

Write the missing *p*'s. Trace the words. Copy the words.

al habet hy hen hone

roblem ha ened ark

PARENT TIP: Note that *ph* makes an */f/* sound in *alphabet*, *hyphen* and *phone*. Make sure your child notices the spelling of *happened* which uses the suffix *-ed* to show past tense.

Practice

Trace

pP pP pP pP pP pP

Trace the labels. Colour the diagram.

Park Equipment Map

Write the sentence.

Pick a perfect spot for Poppy's party.

PARENT TIP: This diagram is a plan or overhead view of a playground. Point out that this sort of drawing is useful to work out how close items are to each other in a space and where things will fit. Have your child write an X on the diagram at the spot they pick for the perfect party.

Practice

Trace

k k k k k k

K K K K K K

Write

k k

K K

Write the missing *k*'s. Trace the words. Copy the words.

sic pic slic flic

new now s y ey

PARENT TIP: Make sure your child starts with the downstroke then moves back up the downstroke without lifting their pencil and then moves in a clockwise direction to form the body of the *k*. The words *knew* and *know* have a silent *k*. Build on *know* to make *knowing*, *knowledge*, *knowledgeable*.

Practice

Trace

k K k K k K k K k K k K

Trace the labels. Colour the diagram.

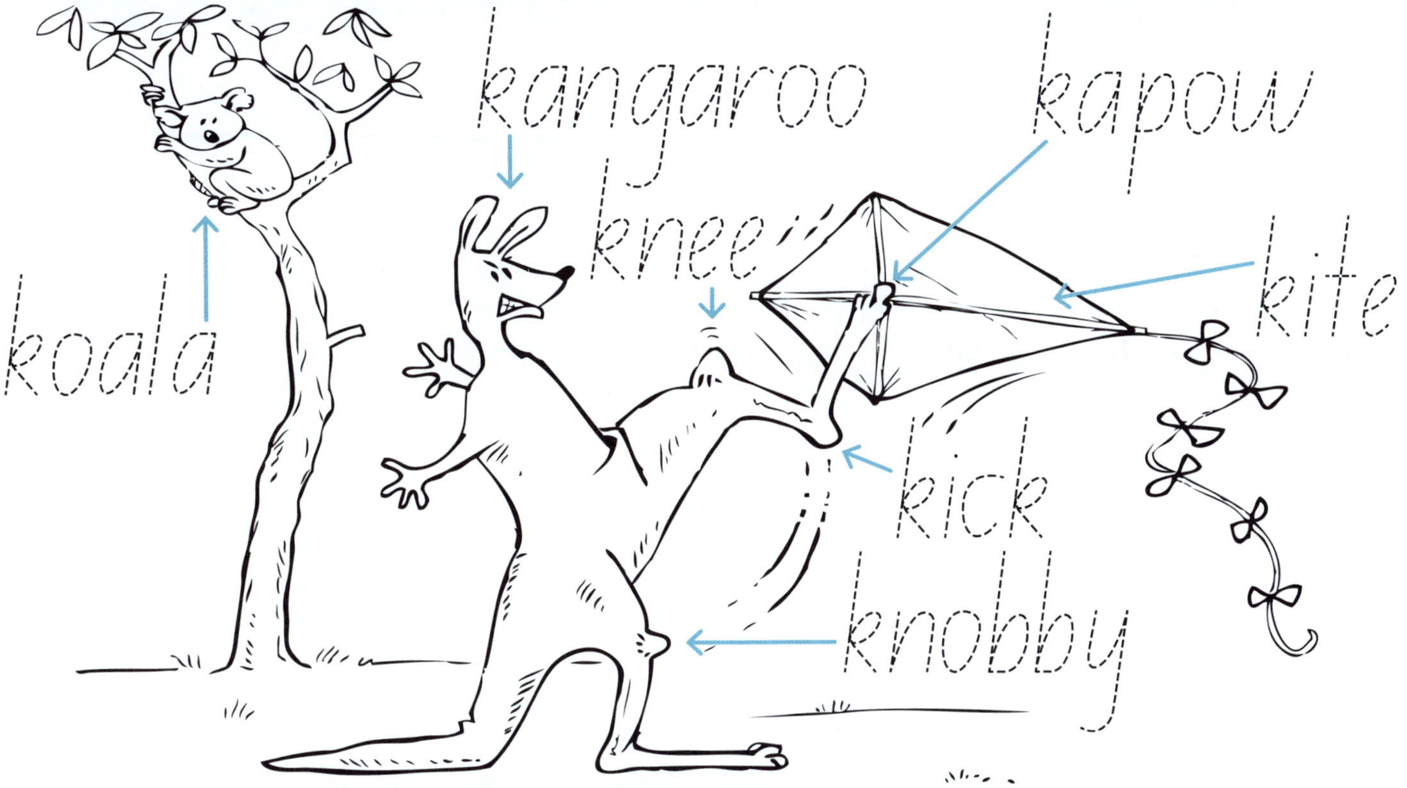

Write the sentence.

Killer kangaroo karate-kicked the kite.

PARENT TIP: Check your child's posture is correct when they are writing. Ask your child to identify words with silent *k* (*knobby* and *knee*). Point out that *koala* starts with *k* too.

Extra practice: clockwise

Write the words.

above alphabet bear

become begin brake

break brittle bush

busy chimp chore

cross door drum fence

flame flick hairy

PARENT TIP: The words are in alphabetical order. Ensure your child uses correct direction and movements for the letter shapes. Correctly forming the letters is important for later development of a fluent, efficient cursive style.

Extra practice: clockwise

Write the words.

hand happened hard

highchair hour hyphen

kangaroo karate key

knew know koala make

marvellous might

money more music

PARENT TIP: Quiz your child on alphabetical order by choosing a different word from any of the previous pages and asking your child where it would be placed in alphabetical order on this double page.

Extra practice: clockwise

Write the words.

near neighbour never

next nice night noisy

nose order party

path perfect phone

pick problem puppy

raft rapids remember

PARENT TIP: Watch that your child's writing style is fluent and comfortable and they are using a relaxed grip. Ask your child to point out to you any interesting spelling patterns they notice. Play with rhyme.

Extra practice: clockwise

Write the words.

river rock same

sandpit score scratch

shape shiver short

show sick sky slick

slippery tame trumpet

whole wrong

PARENT TIP: Point out the silent *w* in *whole* and *wrong*. Find other words with a silent *w*. Discuss the single sound made by the three letters *tch* in *scratch*. Play with rhyme: *hatch*, *match*, *batch*, *patch*, *latch*. Think of other words with *tch*: *ditch*, *fetch*, *hotchpotch*.

Practice

Trace

u u u u u u

U U U U U U

Write

u • • • • u

U • • • • U

Write the missing *u*'s. Trace the words. Copy the words.

t rn b rst h rt t rn

s re • ntil • s ally s re

PARENT TIP: The letters on this and subsequent pages require an anticlockwise movement. Help your child develop a fluid movement that avoids a pencil lift as they make the lower-case letters. Point out that the word *usually* has two *u*'s.

Practice

Trace

u U u U u U u U u U u U

Trace the labels. Colour the diagram.

Write the sentence.

The useless umbrella is upside down.

PARENT TIP: Talk about the *unicycle* being a one-wheel cycle in the same way that a *unicorn* has one horn. Point out that the word *less* at the end of the word changes the word's meaning to the opposite: *useful—useless*, *hopeful—hopeless*, *helpful—helpless*, *careful—careless*.

Practice

Trace

v v v v v v

v v v v v v

Write

v v

v v

Write the missing v's. Trace the words. Copy the words.

dri e li e sur i e li e

e ery oice se eral e er

PARENT TIP: Point out that *v* ends at the top right and does not have a final downstroke like *u* which ends on the bottom line. The final two letters -*ve* can be found in a number of words including *have*, *five*, *drive*. Discuss how the letters *oi* in *voice* make one sound.

Practice

Trace

v V v V v V v V v V v V

Trace the labels. Colour the diagram.

Volcano

Write the sentence.

Mount Vesuvius is a violent volcano.

PARENT TIP: Discuss the meaning of the words in the labels and the meaning of the adjective *violent* in the statement. Ask your child to identify the proper noun.

Practice

Trace

w w w w w w

W W W W W W

Write

w w

W W

Write the missing *w*'s. Trace the words. Copy the words.

fe dre sa dra

hile al ays ho ever

PARENT TIP: The letter *w* ends at the top right. Make lists of rhyming words for *ew* and *aw* (*chew*, *stew*, *grew*; *paw*, *thaw*, *raw*, *gnaw*). Discuss the *wh* spelling pattern in *while*. Brainstorm other *wh* words with the same sound: *which*, *what*, *when*, *where*.

Practice

Trace

ww ww ww ww ww

Trace the labels. Colour the diagram.

Write the sentence.

The wacky walrus wallowed in the water.

PARENT TIP: Ask your child to listen carefully to the sound at the beginning of the word *while* and then to identify the two words on the page that begin with that same sound (*whiskers*, *whale*).
Discuss the meanings of the descriptive adjective *wacky* and the doing verb *wallowed*.

Practice

Trace

a a a a a a

A A A A A A

Write

a a

A A

Write the missing *a*'s. Trace the words. Copy the words.

ch ir p ir f iry ch ir

e rth he rd e rly

PARENT TIP: The letter *a* ends in a downstroke. Make sure your child can write the letter without lifting their pencil using one fluid movement. Point out the *ai* spelling pattern in words on this page and the rhyme they make. *Pair* is a homophone for *pear* and *pare*. Discuss the sound made by *ear* in the words.

Practice

Trace

aA aA aA aA aA aA

Trace the labels. Colour the diagram.

Parts of an Ear

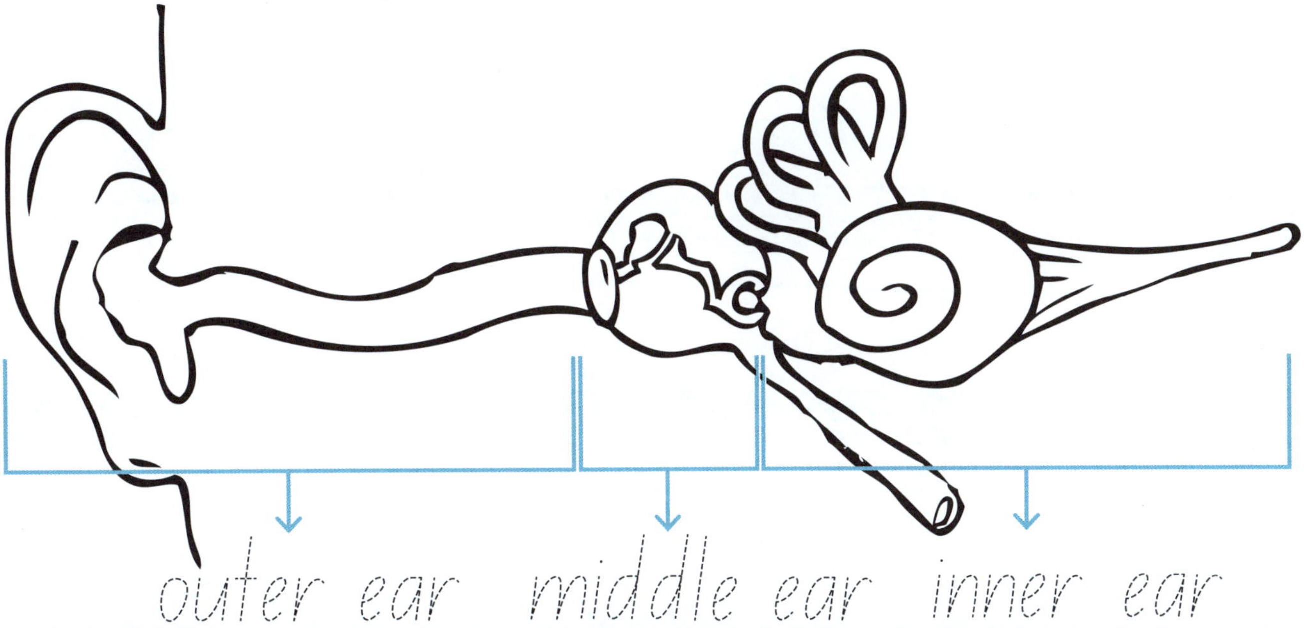

Write the sentence.

The ear is the organ of hearing and balance.

PARENT TIP: This statement is factual and scientific. The labels indicate parts of the ear. The diagram is a cross-section.

Practice

Trace

y y y y y y

Write

y y

Write the missing y's. Trace the words. Copy the words.

deco anno lo al deco

toda ourself ou're

PARENT TIP: The letter y ends with a clockwise tail. Discuss the sound made by the letters oy. This sound can also be spelt with the letters oi (oil, toil, soil).

Practice

Trace

y y y y y y

Trace the labels. Colour the diagram.

Write the sentence.

The yodelling yak did yoga outside the yurt.

PARENT TIP: Discuss any unfamiliar vocabulary, e.g. *yodelling* and *yurt*. Watch your child write the letter *y* and note any difficulty.

Practice

Trace

c c c c c c

C C C C C C

Write

c c

C C

Write the missing c's. Trace the words. Copy the words.

bla k kna k sna k bla k

on e se ond ried on e

PARENT TIP: List other rhyming words for -*ack*. You may also like to make lists for -*ick*, -*ock*, -*uck*. -*eck*. *Once* has a soft /*c*/, as in *city* and *since*. When a word ends in *y* it usually changes to *i* before adding the suffix, with a few exceptions such as when there is a vowel before the *y* or when the suffix is *ing*.

Practice

Trace

c C c C c C c C c C c C

Trace the labels. Colour the diagram.

Write the sentence.

A camel cannot camouflage in cactus.

PARENT TIP: Discuss the humour in the illustration and any unfamiliar vocabulary. Discuss the spelling of the trickier words such as *camouflage*.

Practice

Trace

o o o o o o

O O O O O O

Write

o o

O O

Write the missing *o*'s. Trace the words. Copy the words.

gr w   sn w   f ll w   sn w

f d   wn   sch l   s n

PARENT TIP: Point out the sound made by /*ow*/ in *snow*, *grow*, *follow*, *own* and the sound made by /*oo*/ in *food*, *soon* and *school*. Make lists of rhyming words.

Practice

Trace

o O o O o O o O o O o O

Trace the labels. Colour the diagram.

Write the sentence.

The owl dropped a book down below.

PARENT TIP: Discuss the different sounds made by the letter *o* in each word. Ensure your child moves fluently when writing the letter *o*.

Practice

Trace

g g g g g g
G G G G G G

Write

g g
G G

Write the missing g's. Trace the words. Copy the words.

fri ht hi h si h li ht

thou ht irl round

PARENT TIP: The letter g begins with an anticlockwise movement and then ends in a clockwise movement for the tail. Make sure your child can complete the letter in one smooth movement without lifting their pencil. Point out the igh pattern and the sound it makes.

Practice

Trace

g G g G g G g G g G g G

Trace the labels. Colour the diagram.

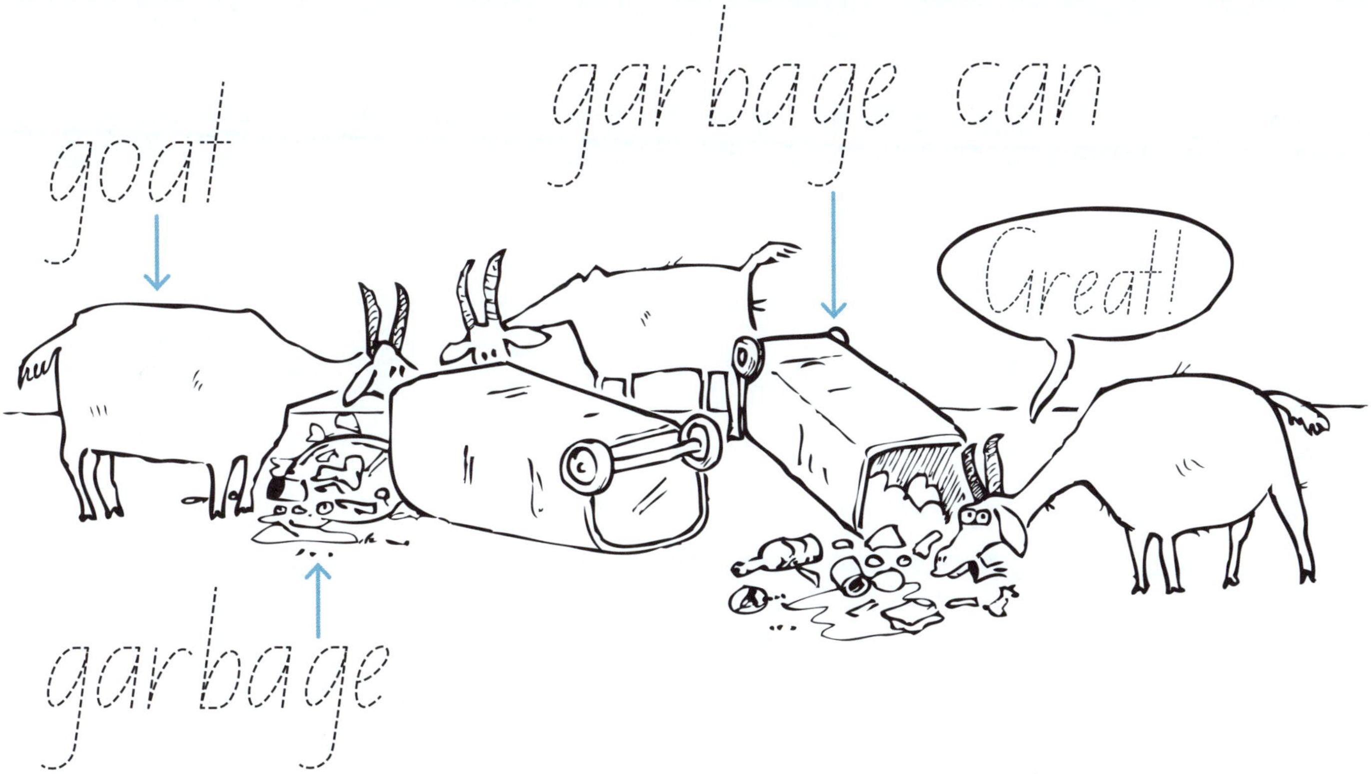

Write the sentence.

A gang of greedy goats gobbled the garbage.

PARENT TIP: The *g* on these pages makes a hard sound. Tell your child that *g* can also make a soft sound like a *j*; for example, *giant, gentle, giraffe*. You could point out that the word *gorgeous* begins with a hard sound and has a soft sound in the middle.

Practice

Trace

q Q q Q q Q q Q q Q q Q

Write

q Q q Q

Write the missing q's. Trace the words. Copy the words.

uiet uaint ueasy

uestion s uare s uat

PARENT TIP: The letter *q* ends with a downstroke. Make sure your child can differentiate *q* from *p*. *Q* is usually followed by *u*. The letters *are* in *square* make the same sound as the letters *eir* in *heir*, the letters *air* in *chair* and the letters *ear* in *pear*.

Practice

Trace

qQ qQ qQ qQ qQ qQ

Trace the labels. Colour the diagram.

Write the sentence.

The quaint quokka took a quiver on the quest.

PARENT TIP: Read the sentence with your child. Discuss unfamiliar vocabulary. Ask your child to identify the descriptive adjectives on the double page: *quiet*, *quaint*, *queasy*, *quick*.

Practice

Trace

d d d d d d

D D D D D D

Write

d d

D D

Write the missing *d*'s. Trace the words. Copy the words.

ri e hi e rai pai

a d on't uring col

PARENT TIP: To form a *d* your child must begin with an anticlockwise movement and end in a downstroke in one fluid movement without lifting their pencil. Watch your child write the letter and observe any difficulty (fluency, legibility, posture).

Practice

Trace

dD dD dD dD dD dD

Trace the labels. Colour the diagram.

Dinosaur

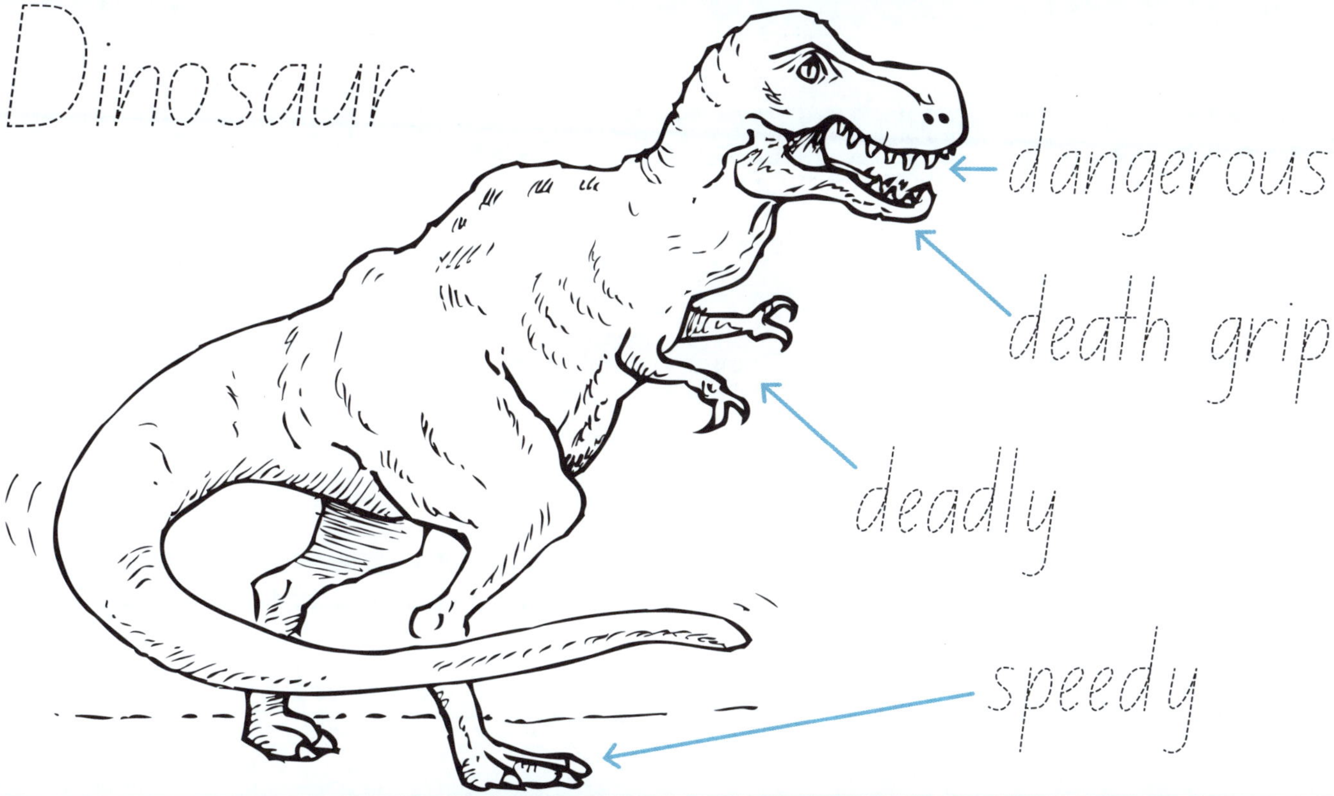

Write the sentence.

'Dinosaurs died,' said Dad. 'They didn't adapt.'

PARENT TIP: Discuss the single quotation marks around what is being said by Dad. It is also acceptable to use double quotation marks (" "). Discuss the contraction *didn't* and the apostrophe to replace the *o* which has been left out of *not* to form the contraction. *Dad* is a proper noun in the text so it begins with an upper-case *D*.

Practice

Trace

e e e e e e

E E E E E E

Write

e e

E E

Write the missing e's. Trace the words. Copy the words.

p d h d m d r d

b tw en nough asy

PARENT TIP: Ensure your child's movement is fluid when writing *e*. Many words have a silent *e* at the end. The silent *e* can change the sound of the vowel in the previous syllable; for example, *mad—made, rid—ride*.

Practice

Trace

eE eE eE eE eE eE

Trace the labels. Colour the diagram.

Write the sentence.

There are three eggs on the leaf.

PARENT TIP: This is a factual text with a life-cycle diagram.

Practice

Trace

s s s s s s

S S S S S S

Write

s s

S S

Write the missing *s*'s. Trace the words. Copy the words.

hadow hock hare

tory omething ince

PARENT TIP: The letter *s* has a double movement. It begins as an anticlockwise movement and ends as a clockwise movement. Make sure your child practises to develop a fluid, comfortable movement.

Practice

Trace

s S s S s S s S s S s S

Trace the labels. Colour the diagram.

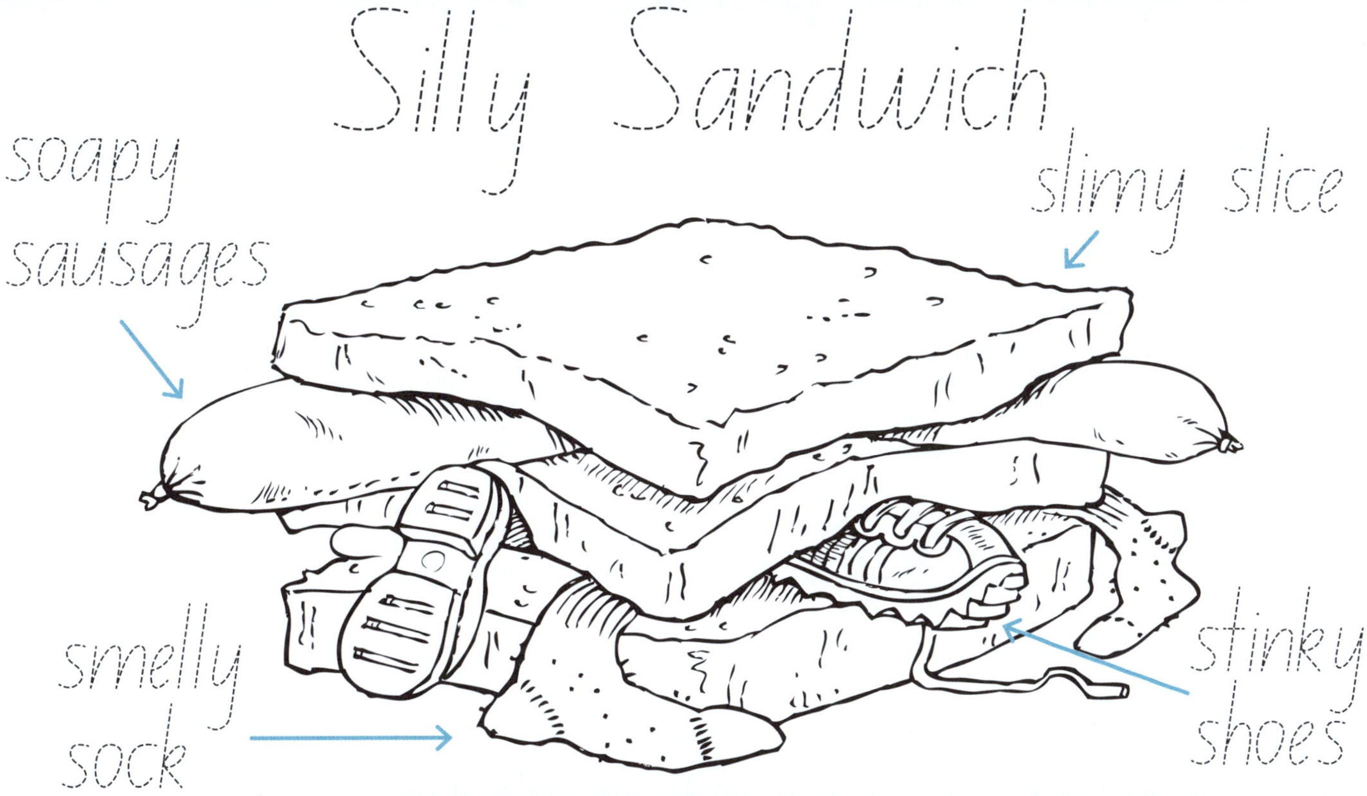

Write the sentence.

'This sandwich makes me sick!' said Sally.

PARENT TIP: Point out the punctuation marks, including the exclamation mark. Ask your child to identify the common and proper nouns (e.g. *sandwich* and *Sally*) and the descriptive adjectives (e.g. *stinky* and *smelly*). Sally's statement is in high modality.

Extra practice: anticlockwise

Write the words.

add always annoy

balance below between

black book burst

butterfly cactus camel

cannot caterpillar chair

chuckle cloud cold

PARENT TIP: The words are in alphabetical order. Have your child read the words to you. Ask them to point out any spelling patterns they notice, such as *ou* in *cloud*. Have them identify the small words in *caterpillar* (*cat*, *cater*, *pill*, *pillar*). They could also jumble the letters in *caterpillar* to make words (only use each letter once): *rat*, *pat*, *tap*, *tape*, *lip*, *pile*, *tile*, *tear*, *pear*, *pare*, *liar*, *rate*, *late*, *pact*, *tar*, *tip*, *tire*, *rail*. See how many they can make.

Extra practice: anticlockwise

Write the words.

cow cried crow cycle

dangerous death decoy

died dinosaur don't

drive dropped during

ear early earth easy

enough every fairy

PARENT TIP: Have your child read the words to you. Ask them to point out any spelling patterns they notice, such as the *ea* in *death* and *easy*. Have your child listen to the sounds in *enough*. How many can they hear? Discuss the spelling of those sounds.

Extra practice: anticlockwise

Write the words.

few follow food fright

gang garbage girl

goat gobbled great

ground grow hear

heard hide high hole

however hurt knack

PARENT TIP: Have your child read the words to you. Ask them to point out any spelling patterns they notice, such as *oo*, *ea*, *ou*, *igh* and *ur*. Watch your child write to ensure their pencil grip is relaxed and not tense and that the letters are legible and fluent.

Extra practice: anticlockwise

Write the words.

lava life light live

loyal middle mule once

outside owl own paid

pair part paw pole

quaint queasy quest

question quick quiet

PARENT TIP: Have your child read the words to you. Give them time to learn the spelling of the words then test them.

Extra practice: anticlockwise

Write the words.

quiver quokka raid

ride rule said sandwich

sausages saw school

screw second several

shadow share shoe

shook sick sigh since

PARENT TIP: Watch your child write the words. Make sure they begin and end each letter correctly. Check that your child's posture is relaxed and comfortable when writing. Watch that their style is fluent and that they are using a relaxed grip.

Extra practice: anticlockwise

Write the words.

slice smelly snack snow

soap something soon

square squat story sure

survive thought three

today took turn

umbrella unicycle until

PARENT TIP: Ask your child to read then write the words. Have your child name the nouns and adjectives on the page. Can your child find four verbs (e.g. *slice*, *squat*, *survive*, *thought*)? Note that *slice* can be a verb (*Slice the pie*) or a noun (*Give me a slice*).

Extra practice: anticlockwise

Write the words.

useless usually vast

violent voice volcano

walrus wallow water

wetsuit whale while

whiskers yellow yoga

you're yourself yurt

PARENT TIP: Have your child read the words to you. Ask them what they notice about spelling patterns in the words. Check that your child understands that the expansion of the contraction *you're* is *you are*.

Trace and copy the numerals.

1 2 3

4 5 6

7 8 9

10 11 12

13 14 15

16 17 18

19 20

Trace the even numbers. Write the odd numbers.

2 4 6 8 10

PARENT TIP: Discuss the term *numerals*. Check that your child is starting each numeral correctly according to the start dots and arrows.

Practice

Trace and copy.

1 one 2 two 3 three

4 four 5 five 6 six

7 seven 8 eight 9 nine

10 ten 11 eleven 12 twelve

PARENT TIP: Discuss spelling patterns in the words for the numbers; for example, the four letters *eigh* that make one sound in *eight*; the silent *w* in *two*; and the silent *e* at the ends of *five*, *nine* and *twelve*.

Practice

Trace and copy.

0 10 20

30 40 50

60 70 80

90 100

Trace the words. Write the numerals.

thirteen fourteen

fifteen sixteen

seventeen eighteen

nineteen twenty

PARENT TIP: Check your child has written the correct numerals for the words. Point out the *teen* at the end of the words.

Practice

Trace the words. Write the numerals.

zero ten

twenty thirty

forty fifty

sixty seventy

eighty ninety

one hundred

one thousand

Trace the words. Write the number.

one hundred and forty

PARENT TIP: Check that your child has written the numerals correctly for each word. Make sure they use the correct number of zeros in one hundred and one thousand.

Practice

Trace and copy. Write the missing ordinal numbers.

1st first

2nd second

3rd third

fourth

5th fifth

sixth

7th seventh

eighth

PARENT TIP: Check your child has written the correct ordinal numbers.

Practice

Trace the numerals. Write the missing numerals.

1	2	3	4		6	7	8	9	10
11	12	13	14		16	17	18	19	20
21	22	23	24		26	27	28	29	
									40
41	42	43	44		46	47	48	49	50
51		53				57	58	59	60
61	62	63	64		66	67	68	69	70
71	72		74			77	78		
									90
91	92	93	94		96	97	98	99	100

PARENT TIP: Check that your child has written the numerals correctly in the boxes. Use the grid to practise counting by 2s, 5s, 10s, 3s, etc. Discuss odd and even numbers. Colour the columns of odd numbers.

Revision

Practise alphabetical order. Trace the letters. Write the missing letters. Draw something that begins with each letter.

Lower-case letter	Upper-case letter	Picture	Lower-case letter	Upper-case letter	Picture
a				N	
	B				
	C		p		
d				Q	
			r		
	F				
g				T	
h				U	
	I		v		
	K				
l			y		
m				Z	

Revision

Sheba's shopping list

- food, bowl and treats
- toys including a ball
- collar and leash
- crate or kennel
- safety harness for car

LOOK HERE!

Before you start, loosen up your wrist and fingers. Roll your shoulders forwards and backwards.

Copy the items on Sheba's shopping list.

Revision

The Incredible Platypus

This egg-laying mammal has waterproof fur, the bill of a duck and the tail of a beaver. Males have poisonous spurs.

LOOK HERE!

Keep letters a consistent size. Make sure spaces between letters are even and that you have left an appropriate space between words.

Copy the descriptive text about the platypus.

Revision

The Ant Explorer

Once a little sugar ant
made up his mind to roam
To far away far away,
far away from home.

Draw a picture.

LOOK HERE!

Make sure spaces between letters are even and that you have left an appropriate space between words.

Copy the beginning of the poem by CJ Dennis. Also copy the title.

Revision

Little Red Hen spent
her time walking about
the farmyard in her
picketty-pecketty
way, scratching for
worms.

Draw a picture.

LOOK HERE!

Stay within the writing lines. Try to judge whether a word will fully fit on the line before you start writing it.

Copy the beginning of the folktale about the Little Red Hen.

Revision

It vanished quite slowly, beginning with the end of the tail and ending with the grin, which remained after the rest of it was gone.

Draw a picture.

LOOK HERE!

When you've finished this page, judge your work. Do any letters need extra practice to make them perfect? Rate this page from 1 to 10.

Copy the description of the Cheshire Cat adapted from *Alice's Adventures in Wonderland* by Lewis Carroll.

Revision

Father Wolf heard
the angry, snarly,
singsong whine of a tiger
who has caught nothing
and does not care if
all the jungle knows it.

Draw a picture.

LOOK HERE!

Show someone else your writing when you finish the page. Ask them what they think about it.

Copy the lines adapted from *The Jungle Book* by Rudyard Kipling.

Revision

All About Me

Use your best handwriting to answer these questions about yourself.

LOOK HERE!

Bravo! You are at the end of the book. Now have a go at writing without the extra guidelines.

My family members' names are

My friends are

My favourite subjects at school are

My favourite hobbies, games and sports are

After school I like to

On weekends I like to

I think I am good at

My family says I am good at

When I grow up I think I might want to be ________

____

____

____

My favourite animals are ________

____

____

One thing I can do to help someone in my

family is ________

____

One thing I can do to help someone in my

class is ________

____

One thing I can do to help the planet is ________

____

At the end of this school year, I hope that my

teacher thinks I ________

____

____

At the end of this school year, I hope that my

family thinks I ________

____

____

One final comment I have for my teacher this

year is ________

____

____

One suggestion I have for my teacher next

year is ________

____

NSW Foundation Style

a b c d e f g

h i j k l m n

o p q r s t u

v w x y z

0 1 2 3 4 5

6 7 8 9 10

NSW Foundation Style

A B C D E F

G H I J K L

M N O P Q R

S T U V W

X Y Z

Posture, paper tilt and pencil grip

Posture

Paper tilt

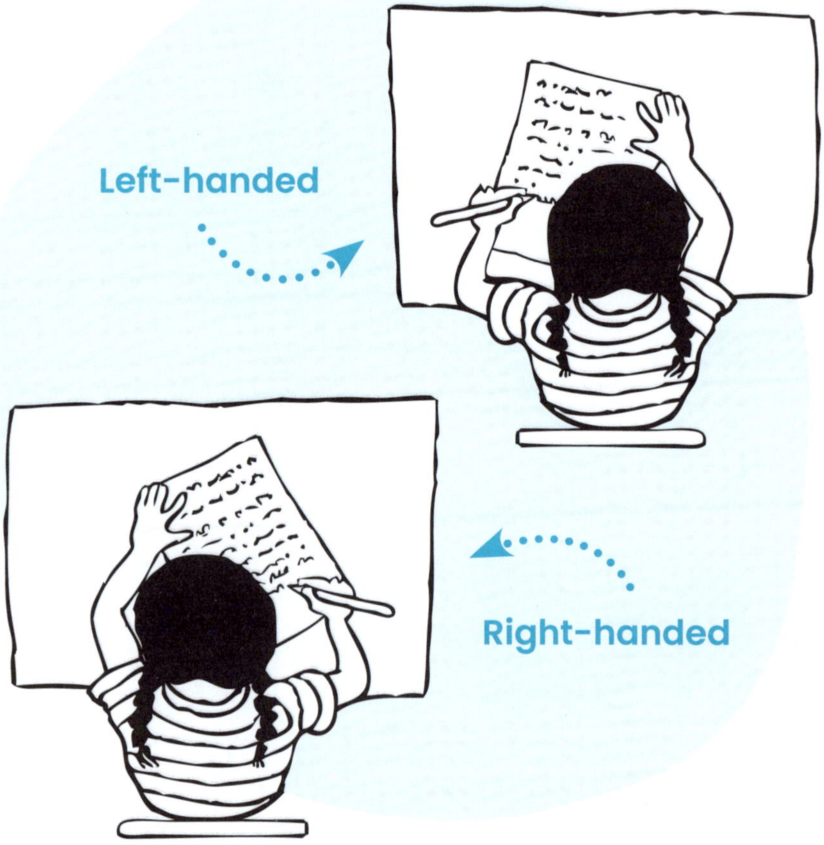

Pencil grip

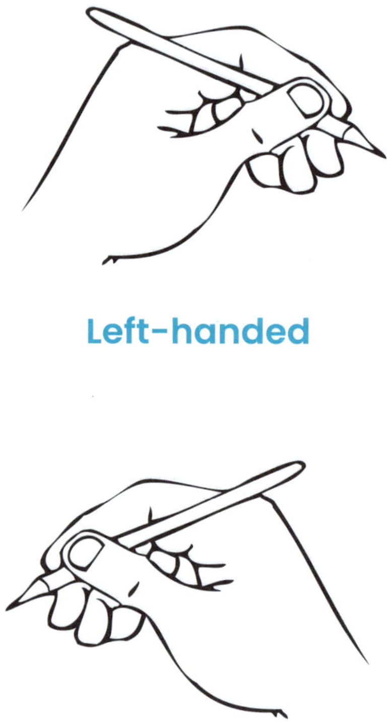